# The Cable Cars

## OF SAN FRANCISCO

*Photographs by Phil Palmer*

*Text by Mike Palmer*

**HOWELL-NORTH**

**N**O ONE WHO has ever ridden on a San Francisco cable car will ever forget the experience.

The freewheeling downhill roller coaster rides, the wild rushes through intersections, the apparently hopeless forays into avalanches of autos, the people who hang onto the outside poles and lean into the street on the curves, the conductors who must remember who paid his fare and who didn't, the gripmen who sweat and strain but who really enjoy it, all belong to the cable car, and to the cable car alone.

The cars have died out slowly since their peak at the turn of the century. The green cars of Powell Street and the red cars of California are all that remain from the glory days before the firequake of 1906. Yet the surprising thing is that any cable cars are left at all.

San Francisco has hung on to these last pieces of nostalgia not merely as an oddity to attract tourists (they are that), but also as a part of the peculiar charm of living on the Bay.

San Francisco is a romantic city—steeped and simmered in the indelible tradition of comparatively easy living. The city is up with the times, without a doubt, but it treats the times differently than do most cities.

The cable car can't keep up with the powerful electric busses which hiss up the city's steepest hills with effortless ease, or even the modern automobile, yet it is still part of the lifeblood of countless thousands who live in and around the Golden Gate. In its unhurried, wandering crawl from one point to another, it seems to refute the mad pace of modern living.

Powell Street cable cars

Some people, among them certain of the city's most influential leaders in years past, have tried to banish the cable car into the land of the five cent beer and steam locomotive.

Partly out of economic necessity the cable lines have been trimmed down. Partly out of pure stubborness some of the harmless lines have been erased, replaced by streetcars and busses. The anti-cable car faction won part of its battle, but the pro-car forces won a moral victory in saving two lines.

The cable car still lives, and although it will vanish someday, the persons who rip out the last narrow gauge tracks will have had a bitter fight with those who love San Francisco and who know the spirit of the Golden Gate City.

A California Street car passes Old St. Mary's Church

The Powell-Hyde car, right, is nearly always crowded by the time it reaches Nob Hill. During the summer, riders on the Hyde Street car can watch the fog blowing over the Marin County hills across the Bay, below.

A conductor pushes
car onto tracks at
Hyde-Beach turntable

# SOME CABLE CAR HISTORY

O N A WINTER NIGHT in 1869, an overloaded horsecar started
up one of the city's steep hills which had been slickened by
rain and fog. Halfway up, goes the story, one of the four horses
towing the car slipped. The car started to roll backwards; the brake
snapped and the horses were dragged down to the bottom of the
grade. Luckily, none of the passengers was injured, but the horses
had to be destroyed.

A horrified witness to the accident was a young man of 33,
Andrew Hallidie, who was born in England but had been a resi-
dent of California since 1852.

Hallidie was fairly well known in commercial circles in 1869
as the owner of a wire rope manufacturing company that turned
out good quality products. Hallidie, like his father before him, was
fond of inventing. Among his patents was one he took out in 1867
for a wire rope suspension bridge. But his most remembered inven-
tion was the cable car.

Hallidie had had some earlier success with mining transportation systems in the Mother Lode gold rush country. He had run
cars from one peak to another over deep valleys, with the vehicles
suspended from a slender but strong cable.

With the thought of San Francisco's horsecar accidents in mind,
but perhaps with visions of financial return prodding him along,
too, Hallidie set out to devise a cable car system for the city.

He took two years to complete the first plans and was ready in
1871 to build a working model. He obtained a franchise from the
city with the proviso that all rights would be forfeited if the line
was not ready by August 1, 1873.

With the financial aid of three friends, Hallidie organized a company in 1872. After the company was born, pledges totalling $40,000 were obtained from various sources, but only $28,000 was ever realized.

First plans called for a line on California Street, but these were abandoned. Finally, a 5300-foot-long section of Clay Street was chosen, and work began in May, 1872.

From that May until the deadline in 1873, this mile-long stretch of street was a scene of bustling activity. No one in San Francisco had ever seen anything resembling what was happening on Clay. A trench was dug to house the cable; supports were put into the man-made gulley; the street was reinforced; narrow gauge tracks were laid, and the channel was covered over to leave only a thin slot at the top.

Finally, in the early morning of August 1, 1873, fires were stoked under the boilers in the newly-constructed powerhouse at Clay and Leavenworth and everything was made ready for the initial run. If everything weren't ready, the franchise would have to be forfeited to the city.

At five o'clock on that eventful morning the summer fog laid in the valleys below the crests of the city's hills. Atop the grade on Clay Street the first cable car, a rickety affair compared with today's models, was resting with its grip ready to be lowered for the test

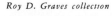

*Roy D. Graves collection*

**Early cable cars consisted of an enclosed trailer and open air "dummy."**

9

**Samuel Clemens, alias Mark Twain, posed in a top hat for this early photograph. Standing at center is Adolph Sutro, prominent early Californian.**

run. Hallidie, his three partners and three assistants waited nervously, then relaxed as they heard the whirring of the cable in the channel.

Hallidie listened for a few moments, then called out, "All Aboard."

Workmen pushed the car to the edge of the grade, the passengers mounted and the first gripman, handpicked by Hallidie, stepped to the controls. He took one look at the grade, and at the fog obscuring the bottom of the hill, then stepped right off again.

But Hallidie walked to the controls himself, turned the old crank style grip and latched onto the cable. The car moved slowly over the edge of the hill and disappeared into the fog. History tells us that it made the trip successfully, as has almost every cable car since.

There was no fanfare, no shouting or romping in the streets at this historic run. According to Edgar M. Kahn, the cable car historian, the only bit of fanfare came when a French baker, clad in

When not running, cable cars rest in the car barn.

nightclothes, leaned out of his second-story window somewhere along the route and tossed down a faded bouquet.

Before long the Clay Street line had become a complete success, leading to the formation of several more companies, some using cable cars exclusively and others using the cable cars on hills and horsecars on flat sections. The most prominent of these was the California Street Cable Railroad Company, founded by the prosperous Leland Stanford, former governor of the state. The California line, which opened in 1878, improved many of Hallidie's inventions. Among the innovations were new and improved brakes, narrower slots to prevent clogging, and better grips, the basic ideas of which are used at the present time.

At one time the cable cars served as nearly the only means of transportation in the city, carrying as many as 232 times the city's population in a single year.

The peak number of lines ran before the earthquake of 1906. After the quake and fire, in which nearly all of the cars were destroyed, many lines switched to electric power. As the new century wore on, other cable lines which gave inadequate service were replaced.

Profit-minded progressives, knowing or caring little about San Francisco's colorful history, tried for years to completely replace the cable cars with busses or street cars. They almost succeeded.

The two lines that are left serve as a concession to the people who, if they cannot remember, at least have a good idea of what San Francisco was like in the wild days when the city was queen of the old west.

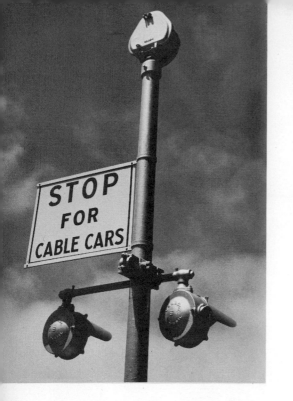

# Plates
# and
# Signs

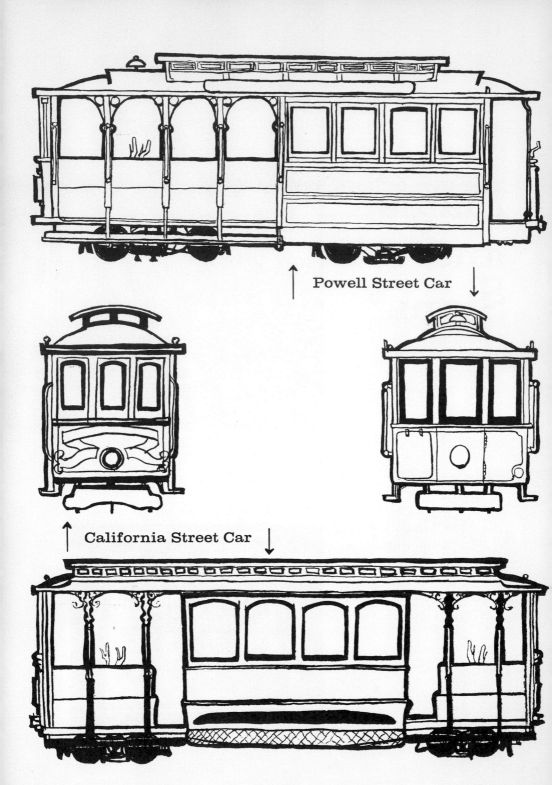

Powell Street Car

California Street Car

# WHAT MAKES THEM GO?

THE MECHANICS OF the cable car system are a mystery even to most San Franciscans. Asked how the cars work, one of them might say—"That thing there, see, grabs onto this thingumbob when the guy pulls that lever, and we're moving, see."

The questioner often doesn't see, for beyond the few facts known by the average San Franciscan is an abundance of detail.

Of the two types of cable cars now running in the city, the Powell car is the smaller one. It is 25 feet long, and is designed to hold 30 persons, not including the dozens of hangers-on during the rush hours.

This smaller car, unlike its counterpart on California, is single-ended and has controls located in the front. It has open-air seats at the front, a small loading platform in the back and a closed seating section in between. Turntables are located at the ends of the Powell line only.

The California car is approximately five feet longer than the Powell cars and has brakes and a grip (mechanism which grasps the cable) at both ends. Switches between tracks at each end of the line make turntables unnecessary.

The California cars once used a grip which clamped onto the cable from the side, but when that line was merged with the Municipal Railway-owned Powell line, new grips were fitted which grasped the cable from the top to correspond with the city owned cars.

The operation involved between the grip and the cable is in theory simple, although it took years to finally perfect the mechanism. Between the car tracks, in a reinforced vault called the "channel," runs an endless wire rope at the speed of nine miles per

Front view of the grip and cable.

Side view of grip in the carbarn.

Gripman's controls, left to right, emergency brake, track brake lever, grip lever and the wheel brake pedal.

The gripman pulls on the infrequently used emergency brake.

hour. When the gripman pulls back on the grip lever, the grip fastens around the cable and the car is towed along.

The principle of the grip is eccentric. When the lever is pulled, a plate is lowered which causes two hinges, called dies, to move together and finally grip the cable. When the lever in the car is pushed all the way forward the cable drops out of the grip entirely. When the lever is at a halfway position the cable runs freely through the grip but does not fall out.

The dies, weighing an amazing 260 pounds apiece, have to be replaced once a week in the machine shop of the powerhouse and carbarn, located at Washington and Mason Streets.

Once the grip starts moving, the gripman, and often the conductor, will use three different types of brakes for stopping—the wheel, track, and emergency brakes.

The wheel brake, the most commonly used, is simply an iron shoe which presses against the wheel. Each wheel is fitted with one for a total of eight. On the Powell cars, a foot pedal, operated by the gripman, activates the front set of four while a conductor-operated screw-type lever sets off the back set. On California cars, foot pedals operate both sets.

The track brakes, lever-operated by the gripman, are blocks of pine wood located on the wheel trucks between the wheels. Each of four trucks on a car is equipped with a track brake. Because hard wood would simply slide on the metal tracks, a variety of soft-pine, which wears quickly but grips the tracks tightly, is used. The blocks last approximately four days in summer, but because of rainy weather are replaced after two days in winter.

The third type of brake, and least used, is the emergency. Unlike the other two brakes, the emergency is completely unique to the cable car. It consists of a steel wedge about eighteen inches long that is slammed into the slot between the tracks when the gripman yanks the red control lever. Often it is wedged so tightly into the slot that a welding crew must be sent out to cut it loose.

The cable itself is a partial brake on ascents and descents because a car gripped tightly onto it can travel no faster than nine miles per hour.

The cables, to withstand all the pressures put on them, have a diameter of one and one-quarter inches and are woven of steel strands. They are driven on wheels connected to 750-horsepower motors in the powerhouse. Separate cables are used for each car route—Mason, Hyde, and California Streets.

In the powerhouse the cables travel around two ten-foot-diameter wheels and two smaller wheels which keep even tension throughout the line. One tension wheel adjusts automatically to sudden slacks in the cable, while the other wheel is set by hand to adjust for stretching of the cable that comes with age.

Damage to the cables, while occurring infrequently, usually shuts down the particular line involved for the day. There are two

When the gripman sees this sign he must release the cable immediately.

The cable is kept in place in the channel by pulleys.

Track brakes are soft-pine blocks set between the wheels.

Grips are taken out and replaced through a special door in the front of each car.

Cables turn on two ten-foot diameter wheels in the powerhouse.

kinds of possible damage—a broken strand or a broken cable. In either case, a new section of cable is spliced onto the old as the damaged section is wound into the powerhouse. To repair a broken cable a 60-foot splice is used—probably the longest in the world.

The channel through which the cable runs is centered in concrete blocks set into the asphalt streets. Imbedded in the cement at three-foot intervals are steel yokes which shape the vault while also supporting the tracks. The channel's shape is roughly triangular with the apex at the slot.

Once the cable is out of the powerhouse, it travels along the channel supported by various pulleys, some of which are located underneath the cable, and some on top. The pulleys under the cable offer no hinderance to the passing car, since the grip pulls the wire rope up, but pulleys resting on top obviously do present a conflict with the passing vehicles. Depression pulleys, (those set above the cable), are either stationary, which means the passing car must drop the cable, or movable, so that the grip simply pushes the pulley aside automatically.

Points at which the cable must be dropped are marked with painted signs on the pavement saying "Let Go." Unfortunately, the gripman sometimes forgets to let go. When that happens, the

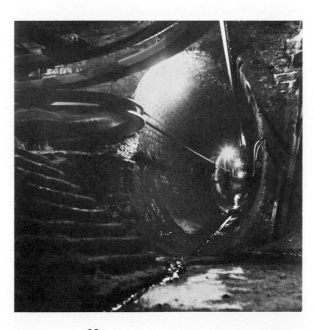

A cable runs out to
the street through an
eerie tunnel

Signs on the pavement, below, tell the gripman
when to pick up the cable. Above, the conductor
pulls the cable up at another pick up point.
At right, a conductor unlocks a turntable.

The Powell and Market
turntable, above.
At left, cars are
maneuvered by tractors
in the carbarn.

Above, a Hyde Street car
travels down Washington
past the carbarn.
At left, a Powell-Mason
car leaves the barn.

Cars rest on top floor
of the carbarn.

moving grip hits a device which rings a warning bell, and a moment later the cable is forced out of the dies by a bar in the channel. The damage caused by this type of accident is probably the most common cause of broken strands.

At the only intersection of the car lines, atop Nob Hill at California and Powell, the bell and bar device is used to keep the Powell grip, which holds the lower cable, from slicing the cross cable in two. When the cable is dropped, the car must coast on its momentum past the danger point. The small shack with the green and red lights on the corner at this intersection serves the purpose of warning the Powell car when it's safe to rumble up the hill, drop the cable and continue across without interference from other traffic.

Once the cable has been dropped, it is picked up in one of two ways. Either a dip built into the street lowers the car closer to the cable, or the conductor must pull on a lever in the street to draw up the rope. At both points are signs saying "Take Rope."

The turntables, located at the ends of the Powell line and its branches, are simply wooden platforms which turn on steel rollers underneath the street.

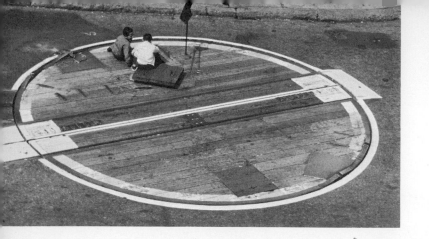

Maintenance crews gain
access to turntable
bases through doors
in the top.

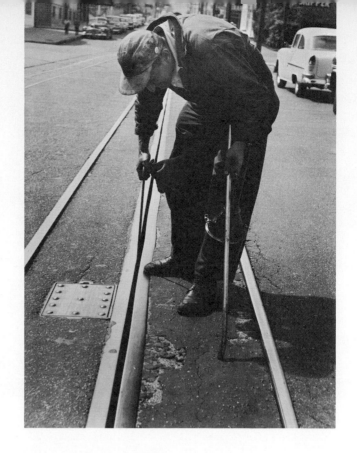

Cables and pulleys must be
lubricated constantly to
keep them in running
condition.

Every July 4, a bell ringing contest for gripmen takes place in Union Square. Bands provide holiday music and San Franciscans turn out by the hundreds to watch the finalists in the contest. The car used is a retired one, now mounted on rubber tires and equipped with a gasoline engine.

Hyde Street car,
at right,
on Jackson

# THE POWELL LINES

**P**EOPLE TAKING THEIR first cable car trip usually embark at the start of the Powell lines. The turntable at the intersection of Powell, Market and Eddy is the boarding point for either the Mason or Hyde cars. The two lines travel on Powell for several blocks, diverge at Jackson and follow parallel routes which both end just a few blocks from Fisherman's Wharf.

During the noon hour and the afternoon rush hours there's usually quite a crush at the Market street turntable; at these times it's often impossible to get a seat on a car anywhere between Market and the top of Nob Hill.

Since it's difficult enough even to find an outside handhold during the peak hours, family groups are better off traveling the Powell line in the mid-morning or evening. Note, too, that women and children are not allowed to hang on the outside—and will miss the views if they have to stand or sit inside the car. To see how busy things can get, study the picture on page 35.

33

The car passes Ellis, one block from Market. At right, a total of nine cable cars seen on Powell during the rush hours.

Powell cars are usually full by the time they reach O'Farrell.

The car travels up Powell, stopping at Ellis, edge of the Tenderloin, and then at O'Farrell, where Al Jolson lived on free lunches from a since-disappeared bar—in the days before he was a star.

The car reaches the jam-packed pipe-stem, Geary, and everybody who has gotten on after Market is hanging on the outside. Many have to stand inside. At Geary is the huge underground Union Square garage, and up the street on the left the city's two big play-houses, the Curran and the Geary, sit side by side. More than one confused theater-goer has bought tickets for a musical comedy at one place and wound up watching a psychological drama at the other.

The car starts up again, moving past the St. Francis Hotel where the doorman and cab drivers never flinch as the Market-bound cable cars brush past their beltlines. Outside Union Square, the Gray Line sightseeing busses are filled with tourists getting their first look at a cable car.

The next stop, Post and Powell, is one of the city's busiest intersections. Within a few blocks are many of the city's best-known department stores, including I. Magnin, Macy's, Saks Fifth Ave., the White House, and City of Paris. The huge highly decorated medical center known simply as 450 Sutter is nearby. Shops displaying books, furniture, painting, sculpture and objets d'art from around the world, and restaurants such as Omar Khayyam's, Moar's and Bernstein's all are found in this comparatively small area.

The car starts up again, reaches Sutter, then begins the final ascent up Nob Hill. At Bush and Pine, autos always wait for cable cars to pass by, never arguing because even gripmen aren't exactly sure where their brakes will stop the cars.

On Pine, the gripman stares anxiously at the signal-house atop the hill, waiting for the green light. When he gets it the car rushes up the final stretch of hill, lets the cable go and freewheels across the intersection. Two blocks down California is Chinatown.

The car rests momentarily at the California intersection then coasts to the cable pickup spot at Sacramento. Here begins the bay-window and high-rise apartment district through which the cars travel for the rest of their routes.

The next cross street is Clay, which, like California, gives a good view of the Bay Bridge and Oakland. The car goes down Powell and passes through the edges of Chinatown, then charges past Washington and finally makes a left turn on Jackson. On Jackson is one of the city's strangest sights—three cable car tracks and two cable slots. Since cable traffic is one-way up the street, cars on each Powell branch—Mason and Hyde—use one outside rail and share the middle one.

The Mason and Hyde cars branch off here. The Mason goes up Jackson one block, then turns right, or north, and ends up just three blocks from Fisherman's Wharf at Bay and Taylor. The Hyde car continues on Jackson for four more blocks, turns right on Hyde and travels toward Aquatic Park. The Hyde turntable is just four blocks from Fisherman's Wharf.

**A pause at Bush Street before crossing Pine and reaching the top of Nob Hill.**

The Mason car, probably more popular because it ends up closest to the wharf, goes past Jackson, Pacific, then over Broadway, which -is encased for several blocks in a well-lit concrete tunnel.

Both cars, before dipping down to the waterfront travel across Russian Hill. Almost as famous as Nob and Telegraph, this hill is historic in the city's past. Lynchings were once common on this mountainette now covered with rows of razor-back buildings. The Russian cemetery that purportedly existed on the hill probably had the finest view of any burial ground in the country. The view is still good enough for an extra $25 rent.

Artists and millionaires often live side by side in Russian Hill's delightful clutter of bay-windowed wood-frame buildings and towering, expensive apartments.

After a long climb up a steep grade, the Powell cars reach Nob Hill and the intersection with the California line. Notice the Sir Francis Drake hotel behind the car and the signal house on the corner.

Another view of Nob Hill. The Powell car crosses
the intersection while the California car waits in the
middle of traffic. The Ferry Building and the Bay
Bridge supports may be seen in the background.

Past Nob Hill, Angel Island and the Bay are visible.

Ahead of the cable cars is a view of the Bay, with perhaps an aircraft carrier or submarine to break the never monotonous patterns of colors from pink to green to blue. If you're lucky you'll see the fishing fleet flocking back to the home wharf, with the gulls trailing behind.

The Mason car passes Union and suddenly at Filbert is the view of Telegraph Hill on the right. The top of this hill was once the site of a semaphore used to inform the lowlanders that ships were sailing through the Golden Gate.

Now, instead of a semaphore stands probably the most famous landmark on San Francisco's skyline—Coit Tower. The tower was erected by Lillie Hitchcock Coit in 1933, a lady remembered now for a slight eccentricity concerning fires. She loved to chase after fire-wagons and, clad in a fireman's outfit of black skirt, red blouse and helmet, watch the city's numerous blazes.

Telegraph Hill, in the last century, was famous for its racy nightclubs. Later a generation of artists and writers comprised most of the hill's population. Then somebody noticed the fine view; today this area is a high-rent section and the former residents are only a memory.

The Mason car turns onto Columbus at the base of Telegraph Hill.

At Filbert the cable car riders can sometimes smell the subtle odor of garlic and guess rightly that this is the edge of the city's sizeable Italian section, North Beach. An estimated 75,000 Italians live in this area which spreads out on both sides of Columbus Avenue. An old-world atmosphere pervades much of this section.

The Mason car makes a half-left turn onto the diagonal Columbus and travels a little over a block before turning right onto Taylor.

A prominent sight on Columbus is the green-and-white night-club, Bimbo's, removed from the entertainment district but boasting some of the city's top acts.

Across the street from Bimbo's is Skipper Kent's, haven for frustrated South-Sea islanders. The cable car passes the back of

A cable car prepares to turn off Columbus onto Taylor Street. Note the pulley access plates on the curve.

Spires of St. Peter and Paul's church.

Coit Tower dominates Telegraph Hill view.

The conductor signals turn from Columbus onto Taylor. Bimbo's is behind the car.

this Polynesian-motif restaurant on Taylor, then coasts onto one of the two "forgotten turntables" at Bay Street.

Just five short walkable blocks northwest of Bay and Taylor is the third turntable at the end of the Hyde line. This line ends in a dirt lot at Hyde and Beach, just across the street from one of the city's favorite restaurants, the Buena Vista. This rendezvous for San Franciscans introduced Irish Coffee to the United States several years ago.

Three other attractions are near by—Fisherman's Wharf, four blocks away; the Maritime Museum, and Aquatic Park. Just a short walk from the turntable, Aquatic Park was built by the W.P.A. in the late 1930's in the shape of a large ship at anchor. Among its features are an 1850-foot-long pier and an excellent sea level view of the Bay. The Maritime Museum, a two-story white building, contains historical items dealing with ships and the seafaring life.

Hyde street directly above the Bay is one of the steepest sections of well-traveled street in the city. As the passenger looks back down the hill he can see a panorama which includes the Golden Gate Bridge (with mountains of fog rushing into the Bay on summer afternoons), Alcatraz Island, Marin County, and the highest mountain in the immediate area, Mt. Tamalpais, as well as Angel Island and the Bay itself.

Occasionally a cable car going up this grade doesn't make it the first time, which usually necessitates a trip back to the bottom before the second try.

The route back to Powell is four blocks west of Mason where it goes left and down to Powell.

Cable car is about to leave turntable at Bay and Taylor Streets. Bright lights are Fisherman's Wharf.

A view of the Hyde turntable at night.
Car lights are powered by batteries
under the seats.

The view from Hyde above the turntable is spectacular,
even when Golden Gate Bridge is nearly obscured by fog.
On opposite page, sailors board the car at the terminal, top left,
and a car races around a curve onto the turntable.

The view down Hyde Street to the Bay and Alcatraz is seen at left. Below, the Hyde car passes along a nostalgic tree-lined block on Russian Hill.

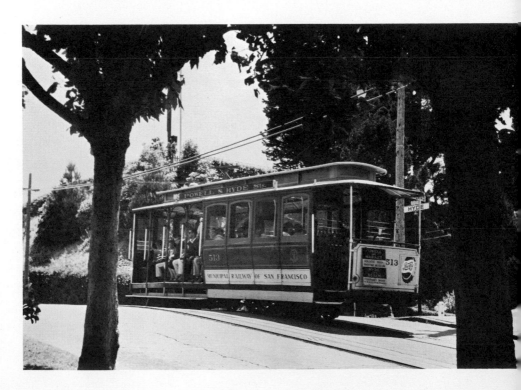

Hyde Street car reaches top
of Russian Hill, left.
Above, and right, Powell Street
cable cars.

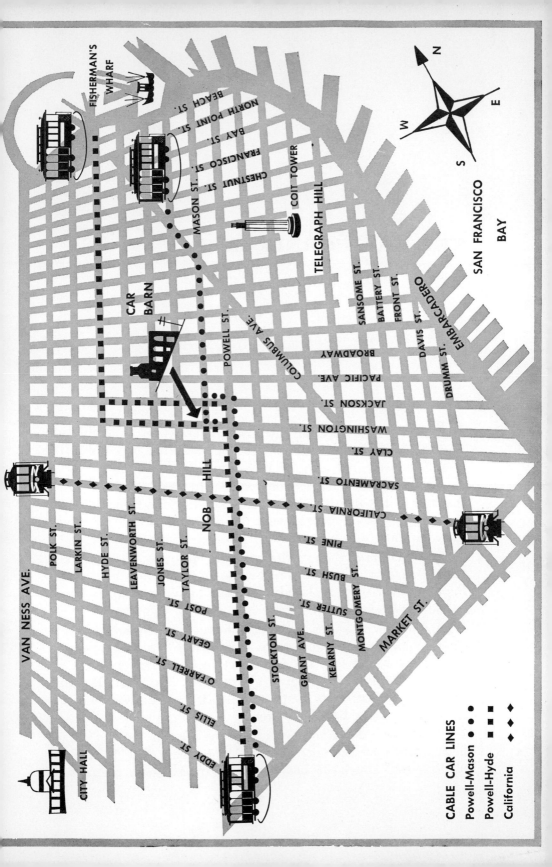

N

E

S

W

SAN FRANCISCO
BAY

FISHERMAN'S
WHARF

BEACH ST.
NORTH POINT ST.
BAY ST.
FRANCISCO ST.
CHESTNUT ST.

COIT TOWER

TELEGRAPH HILL

CAR
BARN

SANSOME ST.
BATTERY ST.
FRONT ST.
DAVIS ST.
DRUMM ST.
EMBARCADERO

BROADWAY
PACIFIC AVE.
JACKSON ST.
WASHINGTON ST.
CLAY ST.
SACRAMENTO ST.
CALIFORNIA ST.
PINE ST.
BUSH ST.
SUTTER ST.

MASON ST.

POWELL ST.

COLUMBUS AVE.

NOB HILL

VAN NESS AVE.
POLK ST.
LARKIN ST.
HYDE ST.
LEAVENWORTH ST.
JONES ST.
TAYLOR ST.
POST ST.
GEARY ST.
O'FARRELL ST.
ELLIS ST.
EDDY ST.

STOCKTON ST.
GRANT AVE.
KEARNY ST.
MONTGOMERY ST.

MARKET ST.

CITY HALL

**CABLE CAR LINES**

Powell-Mason ● ● ●
Powell-Hyde ■ ■ ■
California ◆ ◆ ◆

# THE CALIFORNIA LINE

STARTING OUT at the three-way intersection of California, Drumm, and Market streets, the California line, unlike the Powell routes, is curveless for its 1.5 mile distance.

Partly hidden behind a controversial freeway two blocks from the start of the line is the old Ferry Building. Though the ferries are gone, and some people want the structure torn down, it, like the cable cars, has a great following of defenders.

Down Drumm, though, the wreckers are busy. The crumbling old buildings which used to house the produce companies are being torn down, to be replaced by a costly high-rise complex known as the Golden Gateway.

Among the pleasures of the California street trip are the views of the widely varied downtown architecture. As one travels up from Market, the first striking structure is on the right, at the corner of Davis—the dark gray, glass-layered Bethlehem Building. On the left at Battery is the John Hancock Building, with its black walls rising above handsome arches.

At Sansome one is in the midst of the financial district's dignified architecture; the next street is Montgomery, the "Wall Street of the West." Down this busy street toward Market is the 31-story

58

Russ Building, a skyscraper in a city that has few because of memories of the 1906 earthquake.

Here the red and gold California car starts its steep climb up Nob Hill. At Kearny comes a quick glimpse of Coit Tower on the skyline to the right. The green-windowed International Building is on the corner to the left.

A tall pagoda signals that the next stop is Grant avenue, Chinatown, and the center of the largest Oriental population outside of Asia. At the intersection, besides the pagoda, are the Old St. Mary's

A California car passes through the financial district, left. Above
a car passes Kearny Street with Coit Tower in the background.

Church, built more than 100 years ago, and St. Mary's Square
which, like Union Square, is a park atop a garage.

After Stockton Street is the steepest part of the grade, and a
breathtaking view of the Bay Bridge and the cities across the
water. Then comes Powell, the cable intersection, and the Nob
Hill plateau. On either side of California are two of the city's
larger hotels: the Fairmont on the right and the Mark Hopkins on
the left.

Two contrasting views of Grant Avenue and internationally famous Chinatown.

The Mark, always engaged in a lively rivalry with the Fairmont, has long been famed for the Top of the Mark, a glass-walled bar with a 50-mile view on clear days. So the Fairmont recently constructed its own rooftop nook and a glass-sided elevator which goes up the outside of the building.

Past these is the Pacific-Union Club, a brown mansion erected by a millionaire of the Gold Rush days named James Flood. It was one of the few notable downtown structures to survive the 1906 earthquake and fire; it's now an exclusive club for men.

The Masonic Temple, a little ways farther on the left, is as severely modern a building as the Flood mansion is old. Anyone peering into the lobby will see some huge, colorful laminated murals which are a brilliant contrast to the cold grey of the exterior. Across the street are the English Gothic arches of Grace Episcopal Cathedral.

The car descends from Nob Hill to a predominantly residential district with more bay window architecture. At Polk street, a block from the end, is an interesting shopping district selling such things as antiques, yarns, Japanese art materials, records, etc.

At Van Ness avenue, known as "Auto Row," the cable car makes an abrupt stop—appropriately, at the street where are sold those self-powered machines which are partly responsible for the demise of most of the cable car lines.

The end of the line. That's what the cable cars may be headed for in the not-too-distant future, when the bright little conveyances may be just a memory to the present "younger generation," who will be able to recall with a wistful look the Good Old Days, when the City by the Golden Gate still listened curiously to the sound of the cable rumbling under the streets.

At rght, the view down California Street from Nob Hill. The Southern Pacific sign has been removed